CURE FOR A HUNGRY EMOTIONAL MIND

BADASS TECHNIQUES TO BLAST CRAVINGS OF JUNK FOOD

PUBLISHED BY:Mayur Ghate

This book has been crafted with dedication and passion to enrich the lives of those who, like me, seek to transform their health and well-being. Even those content with their current state can benefit by applying its techniques to other areas where they face challenges. This book does not aim to criticize anyone's dietary habits or choices. Instead, it serves as a companion, guiding readers toward a deeper self-awareness and awakening their true potential.

Table of Contents

Acknowledgements

I sincerely express my gratitude and love for my dear mom and dad, without whom I won't be experiencing this beautiful world. I am eternally indebted to them.

My gratitude also goes to my mentors Mr. Mitesh Khatri, Mrs. Indu Agrawal and Mr. Imran Baig who, through their teachings and motivation, brought an entirely new awakening to me.

To Mr. Jarupala Rajkumar and Mr. Phalak Phogat for reviewing this book.

Last but not least, I also owe myself gratitude for taking the decision to share my success journey in book form to the world to add value to the lives of people.

Introduction

Hello, my dear reader, let me first give you a brief introduction about me. I'm Mayur Ghate, a fitness enthusiast, currently pursuing my PhD at the Indian Institute of Technology, Roorkee (IIT Roorkee). My passion for daily workouts and healthy diets has made me strong and a keen learner. Apart from pursuing my PhD, I'm a professional Handwriting Analyst and Graphoanalytical therapist which I learnt under the guidance of my mentor Mr. Imran Baig. I'm also an NLP and Ho'Oponopono plus EFT practitioner which I learnt from my marvellous mentors Mr. Mitesh Khatri and Mrs. Indu Agarwal. Under the motivation of my mentor Mitesh Khatri, I have been pushed to present my success in front of the world. I'm now finally presenting my own fitness journey through which I have attained my desired body shape. Beating the cravings for junk food has become a challenge for people; people are frustrated with being overweight. This has put tremendous pressure on them and has severely impacted their confidence, self-esteem and most importantly, their identity. Well like you, I have tried every possible food item in my life except smoking, drinking, or any other intoxication. Many of my friends have asked me about the kind of diet I follow and my routine. I do share, but they are unable to stick to the diet consistently. There is plenty of knowledge available on various social media platforms about food and health, but people don't have the right techniques to take action and achieve their desired body shapes. I was also at the same place a few years ago until I changed my mindset regarding my food choices. Yes, my dear friend, I worked on my mind first and automatically, my food choices were taken care of. I proved to myself that before exercise, before choice of healthy food, my mindset matters a lot. Initially, I struggled a lot in bringing myself onto the right path, but small efforts did what was unimaginable. I was on autopilot mode in following what I desired. Finally, after three years of consistency, I'm sharing the techniques and strategies I used compiled in this book you are holding in your hands that will help you achieve your dream body.

The book is written in such a manner that you will get an in-depth knowledge of why the cravings are irresistible and why the techniques work like magic. Well, before using the techniques, it's essential to search for culprits, catch them, and kill them. It is in this way that the chapters are written. This book essentially contains five chapters of three parts. Chapters One and Two deal with emotions and beliefs that govern our food choices and how to recognise them. Chapters Three and Four deal with selectively removing the cravings for junk food and also releasing the emotions that trigger them. And finally, Chapter Five teaches you to live your life with the newly installed emotions. So with an open mind and a smile on your pretty face, fill yourself with positivity and begin your transformation journey.

Chapter 1

The connection of cravings with mind and emotions

Understanding the background of food cravings

Let's begin with the journey of understanding how our mind and emotions influence our cravings. We perceive the world through our five senses, interpret, analyse, and then make decisions or choices. These are the same five senses that serve as triggers for having something or making our move. For example, if your favourite food is kept in front of you on the table, it becomes an automatic response to just gulp it. Similarly, the smell of the food, the taste of the food, and even listening to someone talk about your favourite food item can trigger the urge to have it. In simple words, our senses either alone or in combination, send sensory signals to our brain. After the inherent processing by our brain, a choice is made that matches our hunger, or to be precise, our desire. Please note that here, I'm not referring to the condition of extreme hunger where the body prefers to have whatever is there in front of it, but the special conditions where you don't find yourself really hungry but still want to have that food item. Yes, you read right. These are special conditions because at a given time, you feel the urge and it satisfies your hunger emotion. But is it really only the senses working to instigate your urges? Let's understand. Imagine you had an elaborate meal and you are now full, will you still have your favourite sweet even if it's offered by your loved one? Think for a few seconds so the answer can come in. Some of the possible reactions from your side would be you getting angry with your loved one. In the worst case, that loved one can become your enemy if he/she persists or forces you to have your favourite sweet. In other words, "you are not in the mood to have it". The mood by its official meaning is the predominant feeling or emotion at a given particular state. So basically, we operate at different levels of mind to perform any action.

The Leader of all emotions-Pleasure

Mind is a non-physical intangible component present in us and governs our habits and behaviour. It is our mind that makes anything our favourite and anything our dislike, which has been programmed with certain triggers. If anything gets programmed in a favourable manner, it becomes a pleasure for us and we like it. Food items that are not good for the health/body are also consumed effortlessly if the mind finds pleasure in having them. Now, let's explore the strongest emotion that everyone wants to feel in this world- the emotion of pleasure. You will understand this by the most common example. Most of us have a particular time of having tea in a day, without which we undergo some bodily responses. You may be one of them saying, 'I'm tired now, I need some tea to get refreshed and probably get back to my work.' Many of us say, 'as soon as I wake up, first, I need my caffeine kick on my table, only then can I respond to anyone, otherwise don't talk to me, I'm irritated.' I think tea is at the top of all beverages, surpassing alcohol in socialising with people and making friends. I remember my childhood days when I used to eagerly wait for my dad to come from the office to have coffee made by him. On his morning shift, my mom used to boil tea on the gas, and that smell used to make me happy and give me a sense of pleasure. The drinks or food that give you a sense of pleasure, you just love them, you can't live without them, you close the doors of conscience and logic just to have them. There are a hell lot of videos describing the ill effects of tea and coffee on our health, but be honest, how much do you resist having it? I used to say, 'I know it's not good, but I just love it.' I don't have control or rather, I don't want to control it. The fact is that you can't consciously control your habits; they are formed due to your subconscious programming, which is very tenacious to leave.

Look at the people who are diabetic but still crave sweets; their minds give the reasoning that having one won't have any ill effects. Some people who have increased body heat and acidity but munch on spicy foods, thereafter grab antacids to shut the body's response. It's like a child crying out of pain but being beaten to remain shut. The interesting part is that our mind is finding pleasure even though the body is being tortured, which shows that the mind has lost connection with the body. A healthy individual is not one who has abs, but a healthy mind with a healthy body which are connected to each other. Our mind is mainly classified into two types; the conscious and the subconscious. The subconscious is also referred to as the unconscious. Our conscious mind is like our parents and our subconscious mind a child. A child is very receptive and learns from his parents, replicates them and once he grows up, shows the very same traits he learnt. If the parents taught him good values, he replicates them in his behaviour the same goes for bad values. What matters here is what exactly that child is learning. In this case, what our subconscious mind has been programmed for. The subconscious mind understands the language of emotions, feelings and images, it does not understand your words, actions or resolutions. This is why most people fail in their resolutions, their internal programming overpowers their conscious decisions.

The vulnerable subconscious

Triggers

It is a well-known fact that based on our outer experiences, the actions we take, and our brain form neural connections or neural patterns that get stronger with repeated action. The formed neural connections then remain dormant and get activated as soon as we are hit by the same trigger. Trigger is nothing but an event that has directly influenced our subconscious mind from where our emotions and habits emerge. Also, if the trigger never returns, then the neural connections become progressively weak. The classic example is when you learn to ride a bicycle. Initially, you face many difficulties, but as you go on repeating that action, ultimately, that activity becomes effortless. In your school times, when it was to solve a particular math problem, you were pretty comfortable, but if the same math problem is given to you 20 years later, you take a lot of time to solve it. If the neural connections are partially weak, and if in the future, the right trigger occurs, without your conscious control, you are bound to take that action. Chemically, it has stimulated the release of happy and feel-good hormones to make you feel that sense of pleasure. The main point is the final emotion, what you want to feel after having something. You will keep looking for that exact right food until you feel good. If you are feeling neutral or have balanced emotions, you are perfectly ok even if you are standing in front of a huge container of Gulab Jamuns.

Associations

Apart from external stimuli or triggers that instigate us to take action, the second form of powerful programming is association. You must be familiar with some beautiful memory of yours where your favourite song was played and some event happened, like feeling loved, and then, every time you feel loved or listen to the song, you get back your feeling loved emotion. This is the association of events with our emotions. Food items associate themselves with our emotional patterns or rather we associate our emotions with food. Oftentimes, you have experienced that when you are feeling low or not in a good mood, you have an intense desire to have the sweet and that same urge appears which pushes you to have the sweet. When we meet our old school friend, we feel happy, we say, 'let's have a cup of tea.'

Well, the application of association is rigorous where businesses and companies use such strategies to sell their products! If you are in the sales and marketing field, I don't specifically need to mention the examples as you might be aware of how it is being operated. Most of the restaurants have luxurious ambience in order to bring you in the right frame of mind to have the food, no matter what is the food quality over there. Similarly, many foods contain additives that release happy chemicals that make you feel good. In a way, we become hypnotised by the foods we love, and even if we know they are not good for our health, resisting them becomes next to impossible.

Subliminals
I must say we are very wealthy people and we have kept a bulldog outside our mental house. Bulldog allows the owner, family, friends, and relatives who visit regularly without barking, but if a newcomer tries to enter the house, imagine how a bulldog might bark! Now, if an expert tamer who knows how to tame wild animals comes, do you think the bulldog will bark?

Look how your bulldog barks at bitter gourd (karela) and how it tames itself at spicy foodstuffs, ahh yummy. Many a time, you might have noticed that you don't understand the language consciously, or listen to a song of a different language, and you start to feel the emotions behind it. The information when directly passes to the subconscious mind bypassing the logic of the conscious mind. You get attached or anchored to that information, which is called a subliminal message. A subliminal message is that message to which our conscious mind doesn't put up any questions but still, we feel and see the results in front of us. When do we question anything? When do we analyse something? What if we don't analyse something, will we be able to put logic into that? The best example I could relate to is 2 minute Maggie noodles where that 2 minutes played a significant role in their sales. Who has ever questioned the process? But most of us simply accepted and consumed Maggie. In my school and early college life, I loved that yummy Maggie a lot; it was my lifestyle. Back in those days, if mom had not made any food or if she was out of the station, we would say, let's make Maggie, it's just a matter of 2 minutes without much effort. If you are a college-going boy, you would relate to this; how when we were in a group for an outing in somebody's house, our priority was to make Maggie and enjoy it as it used to take hardly any time. Now that I'm into fitness, I have realised that apart from its taste, in reality, it was a powerful anchor, where my lack of time or laziness was anchored to Maggie consumption. Later on, I observed that Knorr soup also has that 2-minute ability to get ready. As such, if you search, you will find many examples of subliminals.

Key learnings to consider
Our emotions play a dominant role in our lives. In fact, in every situation, it's the fulfilment of our emotions that matters most. Whether we want to feel happy, excited or fun, we often look out to mediums in our world to feel those emotions. The medium may be the love from the loved one, salary getting credited to the account, buying a house or a car, enjoying the warm waves at the beach, or having our favourite food. These emotions are triggered by our five senses and repeated stimulation leads to the association of our emotions with that trigger. Once our emotions are associated, then our emotions start influencing us in the form of urges to experience that desired feeling, which is the boss of all our emotions- the feeling of pleasure. As emotions are created on the land of the subconscious mind, anything that seeps into your subconscious mind has the ability to generate feelings without our five senses. Subliminals work in this fashion where they find their way to the infinite mind without the resistance of the logical mind.

Let's work on a short assignment if you don't mind. Identify the food items you are currently programmed to. Identify the conditions that push you to make your move. Once you do these steps for every craving of yours, trust me, you will feel like you are a monk who is aware of what is happening around you. Well, in the next chapter, I will give more clarity on why we are not able to take action despite knowing we should.

Assignment
List or elaborate on some of your irresistible cravings for food items

---

Write the conditions or specific time intervals at which you feel the urge

---

Chapter 2

Recognising emotions and beliefs around cravings

Decode your emotional pattern and ask quality questions

Now the first step is clear that the main driving force behind our urges is our emotions, the next logical step of our action plan is to recognise them. If we don't know the exact cause of our suffering, we won't be able to design and plan the strategies to tackle them or update ourselves so that we rise above our issues. So at this point in time, we need to be aware of what we feel when we are triggered by our "favourite food item". In my own experience, if I don't pay attention to my emotional patterns, they start controlling me and I become a puppet of my own emotions, swaying all day. The moment you get that spark, oh I'm feeling this or oh, now I know this is my emotional pattern, the work is half done. Now, you have a conscious choice of making decisions. It simply means that you have a charge, whether to become a victim or master. While feeling those emotions, ask yourself some questions; why am I feeling this? What kind of emotion am I supposed to fulfil right now? What kind of emotion am I missing right now? Is it really worth living like this? Asking the right questions is an art, and if you ask yourself the right questions, believe me, your life can turn around. Rather than asking frustrating questions like, why can't I control this, ask empowering questions like, why is it so easy for me to control this? Our mind is always ready to give answers, it likes questioning, so keep asking some quality questions and experience the magic.

Change the self-talk

Unfortunately, many a time, in my own life, I have experienced asking an empowering question that also does not get a satisfactory answer. Even if I emotionally feel certain things, I correct my emotional pattern. Again the same emotions come back and say hi to me. For example, I ask myself why it is so easy for me to gain muscles. What do you think I got as an answer? I got a bleak yes and a faint wow. Emotionally I feel good while exercising, while doing cardio, while enjoying my healthy boiled food but still, somewhere, I feel a lack. Now the question is, why am I feeling a lack? Why am I not satisfied with what I'm doing? And to make it better, I'm really not seeing results in reality! When I was deeply contemplating this issue, I discovered a beautiful thing inside me. We all have that beautiful thing inside us, called our self-talk. You may say I don't talk to myself much, I'm not mad to do so, then pay attention to what you talk with others. Well, every one of us is constantly talking to ourselves regarding situations, people, and events, and that powerful self-talk arises from our beliefs that we are holding onto, God knows for how many years. We have framed equations in our mind through our beliefs though we hate mathematics. Here, I will share some of the common beliefs I have encountered while carrying out research on myself and the people around me.

Our common limiting beliefs

The most common limiting belief where most people are stuck is, "If I don't have this, then people won't call me anywhere". I can't accept myself to be alone, I should be accepted by my peers and my friends, I need to "fit" into society. Smoking, alcohol and non-veg food pave their way through this, if not people or any brand, then movies do the work of programming us. Alcohol has the powerful ability to gather core enemies on a single table. Related to this is, "if I avoid this, then people will call me boring". If I'm successfully maintaining a healthy lifestyle, then I will be alone. No wonder, in this world, there is not a single party or get-together that gets over without having food, so food becomes the dominant player in how we are perceived. "If I don't have the food at the party if I have different choices of food, I will be secluded". There is intense pressure on every one of us to be accepted by our friends, colleagues or even family members. We need to be accepted in society to live our lives comfortably among people. Many times, I have experienced disgraceful looks and comments saying I don't prefer junk food or alcohol. Later on, however, I realised that people who commented were stuck in their own emotional patterns and beliefs and the comments were the justification of their beliefs. From now on, remember that anyone who criticises you or comments on you is lost in his own emotional jungle. People who are being lean are not acceptable to our Indian society as they often hear, "hey are you not getting enough food in your house?" This happened to me when I was lean. My dad told me several times, 'don't go out, otherwise people will say we don't give you enough food to eat. But at the same time, while clicking photos, most of us spend hours and hours to get the right pose to look lean, and some of us contract our tummies like Baba Ramdev. Many of us buy oversized clothes in order to hide our bodies, to look in shape. Another interesting belief that resides in our minds is that if I'm lean, people will look at me like I'm weak and incompetent, hence I need to match the standards of society even if I have to sacrifice my health. Many of them wait for the doctors to say, 'now you should stop having this.' Some of them adamantly say doctors do not know much, they are just bookworms. Do you resonate with any of the above-mentioned beliefs about weight loss or weight gain? If the answer is yes, it extends its tentacles into other areas of life too!

Impact of our limiting beliefs about our body

Now, can you see how conflicting beliefs and emotions are hovering in our minds continuously 24*7? This seems to be a minor issue, but trust me, inside there is a high-level storm going on with loads of emotions like guilt, self-criticism, feeling like a loser, feeling unworthy, etc. The most important takeaway from my own experiences is that I started to relate such emotions with other aspects of my life. For example, there was a point in my life when I was not able to control the urge to have fried aloo, and deep down in my heart, I felt like I couldn't control this urge, hence I was not worthy enough. Is this making sense somewhere? Just imagine how a seemingly small issue can have a huge impact on one's state of mind. People, who everyday look at themselves in the mirror, hate their physical bodies yet find it difficult to control their urges, what quality of life are they living? Well, ask yourself this question - if you don't love your body, if you hide your body, aren't you facing difficulties in finding loving people and presenting yourself confidently in society? People who are overweight and are desperate to lose weight are very insecure about their own body shapes. Moreover, when such people look at the lean ones, they feel frustrated, jealous, unworthy, and like failures, that they unconsciously curse their bodies. Now observe yourself when you look at fit and toned people; what emotions do you exactly feel? Positive or negative? The more negative you feel, the more negative life experiences you will attract in your life, which becomes a downward spiral. By now, you must be having the realisation of how such a small thing escalates itself or rather compounds itself to become a giant devil. Compound effect does not just work in stocks and mutual funds, it's a real concept working each and every moment in our lives.

Our next step of action plan

After becoming aware of your own emotional pattern, the second step of upgrading or evolving ourselves is to recognise what exact beliefs we have that are manufacturing such emotions. For example, what belief is stopping you from taking action to avoid a particular food item you know is not healthy for you or at least minimising its consumption? Also introspect other areas of your life where you feel the same emotion, where you know doing that thing will really help you out but still, you are not able to take action. Keep in mind that we don't have infinite emotions to feel; we have the same finite number of emotions in five core areas of life- health, relationships, career, money, and spiritual, only their intensity varies and the time required to come out of that trap depends on how strong the belief is. Let's start the campaign to recognise beliefs by saying your statement and ending with because, like I used to say, I'm not growing muscles because I'm not going to the gym. Here, 'I'm not going to the gym,' is a limiting belief that I recognised when I said this repeatedly. My next action was to frame a statement and chant it like a mantra, "muscles don't see dumbbells or cables, they need weights", hence I got the same results working out in my hostel room as in the gym. Start recognising your limiting beliefs by finding excuses you give for not doing that or the reasons you give for justification, that's your exact limiting belief.

The following chapter will give you some powerful ways to destroy your cravings. I have personally used all of them, and trust me, I am damn comfortable with not having my chocolate or vanilla ice cream, even if it's there in front of me wide open.

Key learnings to consider
The moment we get aware of our cravings, the next step of our operation is to recognise the core emotions and beliefs that do not let us leave our food habits. The most effective and practical way to interrupt the pattern is by asking quality questions (I call them surgical questions) that shake our mental pattern and bring us to awareness. In this way, we can easily change our day-to-day conversations with ourselves which bring a totally fresh perspective. This process, if properly implemented to recognise other beliefs, effectively

breaks that frozen mental pattern. Finding out the reasons we give or the excuses we give bluntly to avoid the task that must be done helps to figure out the limiting beliefs. With all these techniques, you will be able to understand your own beliefs and emotions driving you without your conscious control.

Assignment
Jot down the emotions you feel while having your favourite junk food

---

Some of your beliefs that hold you from taking action

Chapter 3

Blast your rock-hardened cravings

Here, you open the doors to the next step of your action plan where you will have the dynamite to blast all your cravings and stand like a superhuman. The strategies I have mentioned in this chapter, I have used practically all of them, depending on the intensity of my own cravings. In your case as well, one strategy might work for all or you may need a combination of strategies. There is a disclaimer stating that some of the strategies I have used are pretty disgusting, after which I'm not able to have my once-upon-a-time favourite food item. So if you have the same desire or thinking to remove cravings from the roots, then only use them.

Waning like a moon

Can you believe me if I tell you that I deleted rice from my lunch and dinner completely and I have it only when I'm out on special occasions like biryani parties? Well, I must say I used to eat rice in my home in huge quantities. That smell of freshly cooked rice could trap me and tempt me to consume large quantities. Many times, it has happened that I just had rice alone without any curry but pickle, which shows how much I used to love having it. Then on some awakening day, I learnt that in order to be shredded, I should reconsider my carbohydrate intake and should have check on my existing consumption. Well, you know that just knowing something is not enough, you need to take some action, hence I decided to leave rice from my diet, but how? To be honest, I didn't do it from the second day itself. People make this huge mistake of suddenly eliminating anything completely from their diet. Let me tell you, only an Iron Man can do that type of stunt. We don't have to be hard on ourselves, we are here to deal with cravings smartly. I started to subtly reduce the quantity of rice every 2-3 days like a moon waning from full moon to new moon. I reduced the quantity so subtly that my body didn't react to its deficit. When you abruptly stop something, you are literally punishing your body. Remember, right now, your body is conditioned to that particular food, like a baby conditioned to have candies. If you don't give any candies to the baby, the baby will go crying, yelling, and screaming, but if you go on subtly reducing the number of candies by one or two, the baby will hardly notice that subtle difference and will be comfortable. Consider any of the food items you crave and reduce their consumption gradually so that your body is out of the conditioning process.

Taking a U-turn

I had a habit of consuming one cream biscuit pack at a go, sitting in a posture like I'm having lunch, enjoying every bit of it. Those Oreo biscuits filled with cream, yummy, aren't they? Can the earlier strategy be applied here to get rid of this urge? In your case, it may be applied, but in my case, I tried, still the empty wrapper would be left at the end. It was a time I was just pondering about tackling this when I happened to encounter one video on YouTube elaborating on the health status of biscuits and other packed items. I got a bulb on the moment, oh yes, I got a solution. From that time onwards, I streamed a series of videos giving negative information about those packed foods. I deliberately did that for so long until my urge to have the packed foods decreased considerably. So here is the take, the way your mind got programmed to the food, break the program in your mind by tuning into negativity. Start hearing, seeing, and listening to so much negative about the food item that at a point, you are seriously discouraged and you stop feeling any urge.

Making a declaration and stating your intention

Around 2019, I had a belly fat that swings each time I walk or sit. I could feel and see my protruding belly either standing or sitting. Since 2017, I have been mesmerised by the law of attraction and thought of giving it a try. While bathing, I used to say affirmations and visualise that "this water is burning my belly fat". Well despite doing that with great consistency, I didn't get any results. In fact, I was more frustrated, then I started to doubt the law and assumed those who speak of the law of attraction are simply making hype out of it. Well, sometimes the other part of your mind has already been convinced with the concept and does not let you leave it. Has it ever happened to you that you wanted not to believe something, but some part of your mind resisted it? The same happened to me that time and then I dived deeper and realised that one thing was missing in my practice- intention. When you begin your journey to achieve a particular goal, ask yourself, do I really intend to do this? You know what, girls have this superpower of figuring out the intention of boys, no matter what words they speak, or in which tone, what matters is the intention. Similarly, in this case, affirmations were not working simply because I didn't intend it to. If there is no intention, how will I achieve my goal? Then I woke up and declared this following statement- "I hereby declare that I'm an athlete and live in an athletic body, live athletic life and enjoy athletic body." Further, "I intend to reduce my belly fat, I intend to tone my abs in order to be of athletic personality", "I love exercising and exercising is my life, I'm a warrior who has decided to keep moving". Got some kick? How are you feeling just by reading these declarations? I felt supercharged and without any affirmations, I lost 14 kgs in just 3 months! Yes, you read it right, within 3 months, I was in my desired shape, with full-on energy, and as a by-product, surprisingly, my frequency of catching cold was considerably reduced. Isn't that amazing? Many people are scared of losing weight because they feel they will become weak and susceptible to infections. Let me tell you buddy, your body, tissues, and each and every cell are listening to your thoughts, words and feelings, if you declare what you want, trust me, your body becomes what you want. Just try declaring, it does not cost you money, it simply demands some of your time and energy. Kick in and achieve your goal. You are much more capable than you are thinking my friend, you are awesome, you are an energy being, and you are unstoppable.

Finding other alternatives

I successfully beat all my spicy and sweet cravings, but then, what should we have if we leave everything? I got so much clarity about how the world is operating, which means if people want to leave something, they can't because the options available are too less. I believe that if people have options, people will make the best choices by themselves. Well, in the current scenario, most of the working people are also striving for homemade food, and I have seen people begging for homemade food. I want to have just plain dal rice, sitting on the floor with folded legs, please serve me. Still, I'm noticing a huge shift towards vegan culture and organic things. The alternatives to the existing ones are making a slow comeback. I really appreciate the conscious efforts of some organisations which are dedicated to serving people.

Indian culture is inherently rich in wisdom that we don't need to adopt fancy diets at all; we just need to accept our ancestors' food habits which are still there, fortunately. I remember being a Maharashtrian where jowar and bajra bhakris were part of our diet, but slowly, they went missing and were replaced by wheat rotis and white rice. So when I eliminated white rice from my diet, I brought back our old tradition of millet, and today, I'm enjoying them with the same intensity as rice and roti. After the replacement of rice, I successfully replaced roti as well, and now I'm comfortably munching on millets with dal. Yes, without compromising muscles on my body. Of course, you should listen to your body while having or replacing something. I do agree that replacing something takes you out of your comfort zone. Initially, you might also find it difficult to adapt yourself to a new way of living, but please, trust me, later on, you will love the way you feel. Remember, in the previous chapter, I discussed that the ultimate destination is feeling, please allow yourself to feel better and calmer. Allow yourself to create a space of your own, and value yourself and your body. Our cells are working for us, don't kill them in the name of pleasure. They love you, and expect love from you.

We as humans have a natural inclination towards sweetness in our diet and in our life. Nature understands our needs and has provided us with its natural sweetness in the form of fruits. Sugarcane is growing tall for us to provide its sweetness. Most of us love sugarcane juice, right, so refreshing! That brown-coloured jaggery from cane sugar is my favourite replacement for refined sugar. I literally put loads of jaggery in my tea and coffee and enjoy every sip of it. I fulfil my sweet needs by the use of this unrefined sweetener, and at the same time, I have my defined rock-solid abs. As another alternative to refined sugar, I have had rock sugar (dhage wali mishri) and enjoyed its natural sweetness in my beverages and recipes. For common salt, I have entirely switched to rock salt, which gives the same salty touch to food. There are many videos out there saying rock salt and common salt are the same except for some trace minerals present in the rock salt. I asked this question to myself and a few of my friends. Just tell me, if you are alone, how would you behave, and if you have someone with you, how would you behave? You would be a totally different personality, right? The same goes for unrefined and refined; refined always works like a devil and unrefined works like a saint. Obviously, we should maintain the quantity, but you know what, you are not under any stress or guilt when you are having unrefined foods, which matters a lot buddy. When you are not in an emergency, you can comfortably spend your life on unrefined things; your body is quite sensitive to let you know if there's something wrong, you just need to pay attention to your body, that's it. So if you are comfortable and willing to replace some of the refined processed foods, do so by accepting our original Indian food choices. I'm sure you will hardly need a doctor.

Facing a dead-end

This is the most disgusting method I have ever used to remove my stubborn cravings; later on, though, I learnt this is one of the most powerful NLP (Neuro-Linguistic Programming) techniques. I would like to again request you to go through this method only when you are really committed to just getting rid of crystallized cravings. I applied this technique for the unusual craving for pav-bhaji. What comes to your mind when you hear or imagine pav bhaji? That spicy red hot stuff and that round butt-like bread with butter. Wow, amazing yummy treat, right? Well, for me today, it's not, it does not mean I don't have it ever, I just change my programming before having it, because I have programmed myself. With your permission, let me explain exactly what I did. One fine evening, without any reason, I had the urge to have pav bhaji at a local stall. I went there, stood, and didn't order, though, but saw the guys making it. From nowhere, I got discouraged and left, why? I imagined in my mind that red hot bhaji is nothing but the shit of a person suffering from constipation. This is because the consistency of bhaji was like that. What to do to make it better. Naturally, I immersed myself in the smell of loose-motion shit. I was like omg, why is this happening, why is my mind going in that direction? But sooner, I felt relaxed from that unnecessary munching. This worked so crazily, after which I literally could not have pav-bhaji again. I then had to reprogram myself to have pav-bhaji by recalling the tastiest pav-bhaji I had. With this insight, I started to apply deliberately to other food cravings that were troubling me. Soon, I did for jams. There was an industry beside my house whose effluent had jam flavour, so I deliberately started to visit and relate that smell in my jam jar. Every time I opened it, I imagined I was consuming effluent from industries. Guess what happened next? I never had that jam from the jar! This method worked for me very well, but here I'm sharing with you one of the powerful NLP techniques I learnt from my mentor Mitesh Khatri so that you can apply it to blast your stubborn cravings

Step 1: Close your eyes, it will be easy for you to imagine.

Step 2: Imagine any food item like gol-gappe.

Step 3: Assign some arbitrary number indicating intensity from 1 to 10 depending on your cravings for it.

Step 4: Simply increase your cravings by increasing its visual appearance, smell, taste, and feel. Again, assign any arbitrary number.

Step 5: Slowly start decreasing the intensity by imagining nasty undesired aspects like imagining the water of gol-gappe is a little bit smelly. Further make it down by imagining the puri to be soft, not crisp, and assign a number. It should have decreased by now.

Step 6: Take it negative below 1 by imagining there are wings of dead cockroaches in the gol-gappe water and the guy also has just come from the washroom without washing hands, dipping his unwashed hands in the water and serving you.

Step 7: After you are out of control and feeling absolutely yucky, open your eyes and look up to the fan and tease it. Again, reassess your feelings to have it. If it has reduced, practice it until you don't feel any urge, and the work is done!

Keep practicing these strategies either one of them or all when you are neutral, so that when that particular trigger activates your senses, you won't feel any cravings. In the next chapter, I'm going to introduce you to two such magical techniques which will not only eliminate your "on-the-spot cravings" but will release them completely from your system. It's like deleting the files from the recycle bin.

Key learnings to consider
In the current scenario, people have a lot of information available about health, food and lifestyle. There are many prescribed diet plans designed to achieve that desired body shape. However, people find it very difficult to achieve their health or weight-loss goals because they don't have strategies handy that could change their mindset. Rather than working on the outside, we all should work on the inside. The strategy of subtly reducing the quantity of your craved food changes your conditioning over time which changes your actions. When we hear something negative about a person, we change our

perception a bit. It produces a similar effect on our cravings and then we automatically look for healthier alternatives. While most of us are very strongly associated with our food cravings, the experience of nasty events is often successful in breaking those associations into pieces. The techniques of NLP show crazy and long-lasting effects on almost all sorts of cravings by reprogramming the subconscious mind. People find it extremely difficult to have the same food which they once craved for.

Assignment
Assign a number 1-10 for your food cravings before practicing the strategies

____

____

____

Strategies you used for eliminating your food cravings

____

____

____

____

Intensity rating after strategies employed

____

____

Chapter 4

Cleaning up the residual mess

In the previous chapter, I provided you with the dynamite to blast the hardened rock-like cravings, and by now, if you have used any one or combination of strategies, you might have successfully broken the rock. However, the rock when blasted hard, breaks, but the debris remains. Will it be absolutely ok, if the debris remains like that in your mental room? Would you not like to clean up the remaining mess so that your mental room looks clean and elegant so that you can decorate it? Here is the time to clear out the remaining debris, because the debris also has the power to trouble you. The debris is nothing but our lingering emotions.

The ancient Hawaiian prayer

It was not long ago after my learning of the law of attraction when I was pretty unsuccessful in achieving some of my health goals, that I intuitively realised something was blocking my way. I need to find something that should clear all the intervening blocks because, in some parts, my affirmations and intentions were not working. I would like to introduce you to one of those two magical techniques that I personally practiced. One such technique is an ancient Hawaiian prayer popularly called Ho'oponopono. If you are reading this word for the first time, it may sound weird, you might be exclaiming, what this is! I was like what voodoo kind of thing is this? The name might sound very weird, but my friend, it has profound magical effects.

The first time when I used it, you won't believe what I experienced. I had a fever and I knew that the next day, if I missed my workout, I would feel an emptiness within me. I was familiar with this prayer and decided to chant it while going to sleep. To my own surprise, my fever went away in a single night! I have shared my personal testimony on my YouTube channel right on that day. I will share with you a brief history of how this prayer got its marvellous recognition.

Dr. Hew Len, a clinical psychologist hailing from Hawaii islands used this powerful prayer to cure all the patients having criminal tendencies admitted to the mental hospital. It was roughly around 1983 to 1987. Dr. Hew Len was working in the Hawaii state mental hospital. Well, as a student of Ho'oponopono, he knew the magical effects of this prayer, hence he started to go through each of the files of patients admitted to the hospital and started chanting the prayer. The prayer goes like ***"I'm sorry, Please forgive me, Thank you, and I love you"***. Your limiting beliefs may put a question in your mind about what these phrases might do, but to shake the beliefs, it cured all the patients in the hospital. The most amazing part of this true story is, Dr. Hew Len never met the patients physically! Are you even able to convince yourself now? Just imagine how it cured all the patients so that authorities had to shut down the hospital because there was not a single patient left! If they can be cured, why not your cravings dear?

Have you watched the popular movie "The Secret"? If yes, do you remember one great personality who appeared in that movie? It was Dr. Joe Vitale. This man is my favourite, and he literally brought up the desired fame to this ancient technique. Still not getting the feeling of how it would make a difference? Imagine you are a grown-up child and your parents didn't pay enough attention to you during your childhood. One fine day, you come home from your job and as soon as you open your door, your dad or mom is bowing down in front of you saying I'm sorry my dear child for not giving you enough love and care, please forgive me for ignoring you, thank you for being with me for so many years, I love you the way you are, you are lovely my child. When you hear those words from your dad or mom, won't you instantly shed tears and dissolve your hard feelings for them? This is exactly what this prayer does; it dissolves your negative emotions that have been blocked for years.

Let's go through the steps of Ho'oponopono prayer that are giving marvellous results to people.

Step 1: Close your eyes, take a deep breath, and relax yourself.

Step 2: Keep hands on your heart, slowly move in a circular motion as if you are cleaning your heart and follow the script; you may change it as per your problem.

Step 3: Take responsibility for your problem by saying "I take 100% responsibility for my problem, I have created this issue, and it's my manifestation"

"I'm sorry my dear body for not taking enough care of you"

"I'm sorry my lovely body, for ignoring you, keeping you as the last priority"

"I'm sorry my dear body, for putting unnecessary burden on you out of pleasure"

"Please forgive my dear body for all my actions"

"Please forgive my dear, for not considering you as a wonderful gift from God"

"Please forgive my dear body for holding negative emotions against you"

"Thank you so much, in spite of my ill actions, you are still there with me"

"Thank you so much, in spite of my hard feelings, you are working for me"

"Thank you so much for giving me feedbacks and continuously trying to adjust yourself".

"I love you for the way you are"

"I love you for your faithful dedication towards me, keeping me alive"

"I love you for all your responses which are guiding me".

Step 4: Take a deep breath and be in a Namaste position, bow a little bit down and say I'm sorry, please forgive me, thank you, I love you. At last, hug yourself and place your head on your shoulders. Feel the emotion of self-love for some moments, and then slowly open your eyes with a beautiful smile. Check the intensity and look upwards and smile.

When I practiced this for my unhealthy habit, believe me, I cried a lot. I shed a lot of tears as if some negativity is flowing like a river. If you also experience this, please do cry, and let all your emotions go away. You might not cry but yawn a lot, after which you may fall asleep like a baby. Just do it, allow your body to react the way it wants. Don't hold, enough holding for these many years now, open up your dams, let the water flow.

Emotional Freedom Technique (EFT)

As I was exploring more of this healing modality which is already helping me in many aspects, I was suffering from sinus issues and looking to clear up my sinuses by draining the mucus buildup. I came to know about certain acupressure points on the face and other body parts that would stimulate the drainage process. Thanks to artificial intelligence; it suggested videos of facial tapping, and eventually, I landed on the second technique of tapping. This tapping technique relieved my sinus headache crazily within 2 minutes and regularly practicing this technique, zeroed my incidences of sinus attacks. This was a wow moment for me and I started to practice for my muscle cramps, muscle soreness, wounds, and swelling which always gave me 100% results. You by now are excited to know this technique. Sure, that's why I'm here in this chapter to get you also familiar. The technique is called Emotional Freedom Technique (EFT), initially referred to as Thought Field Therapy (TFT). The term EFT was coined by Dr. Gary Craig and was used for healing purposes. It now has been proven that the manifestation of any disease or pain in our body is due to some blockage in the energy fields within us. Science has proven that we are energy beings and we are living because our electric field is working. If by any means that electric field is blocked by our emotions, then we face physical distress. Emotions are nothing but energy in motion, that's why an emotional person is much more powerful than a logical person. This is because emotions carry energy.

Let's get back to our understanding of EFT. EFT is essentially tapping on our meridian points or energy centres. It is the advanced psychology wherein acupuncture has been replaced with tapping where we don't need needles. The same effect can be brought in by our fingertips. It has also been approved by medical bodies as a healing practice. There are 9 to 15 points where tapping is done with our desired script depending on the problem. First, I will list all the tapping points, and then give you my own example of how I exactly practice for my cravings. Before proceeding, it's not a thumb rule to use any particular hand for tapping, you can use either, but usually, we use our dominant hand for tapping.

1. Karate chop point (of either hand)

2. Above the head (crown chakra)

3. Centre of the brows (at the third eye)

4. Side of the eyes.

5. Below the eyes (the bony part)

6. Between the nose and upper lip

7. Between the chin and lower lip

8. At the collarbones

9. 4 inches below the armpits (you can tap both sides) (Refer to the figure for the clarity of the position of points)

Optional points- the outer side of the base of the fingernails except for the ring finger (inner side) and gamut point behind your knuckle of the ring and little finger.

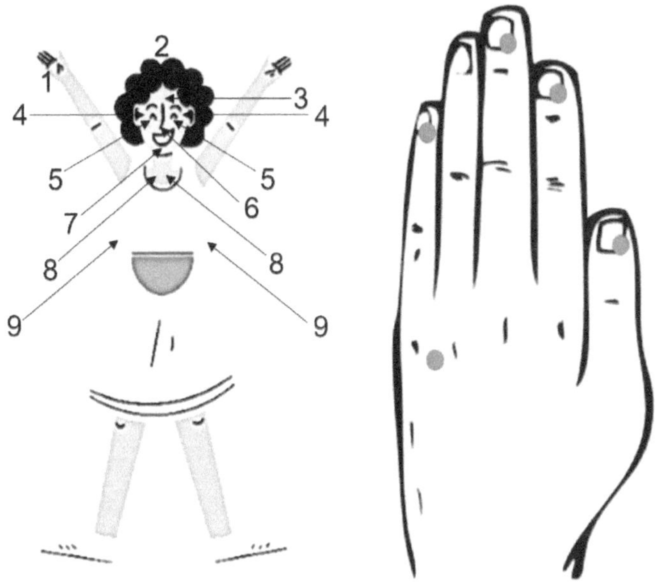

I will now give you a demonstration of how I used EFT for my cravings for ice cream. To begin with, first measure your intensity of craving and assign an arbitrary number by your intuition. Starting to tap on the karate chop point of my left hand, with four fingers of my dominant hand (right hand in my case), I first stated what issue I was facing right now. It goes like "Right now, I'm craving badly for ice cream", "I'm getting distracted by the urge to have ice cream", "I'm on my fitness journey, but finding it hard right now to control my urges", "if I allow myself right now to have ice cream, later on, I will feel guilty of having it". Once you state your problem while tapping, your mind and body come in the right frame to release the trapped emotion. Then at the next step, I said, "even though I'm having an intense urge to have ice cream, in spite of this, I want to love and accept myself exactly the way I'm". Repeat this 2 times more while tapping on your karate chop point. Hence repeat even though (your problem) in spite of this I want/choose to love and accept myself exactly as the way I am. Then following the other tapping points in the sequence, just say this urge of having ice cream, this urge is freaking me out, this urge is distracting me, I'm feeling uncomfortable. As you keep tapping at points, you don't need to consciously choose what to say, you automatically will be in your natural flow. At last, when you reach your above-the-head point, one round of EFT is completed. Take a deep breath and reassign an arbitrary number to the intensity. It should get down. Let's say the initial number was 8, after one round of tapping, it would come to 5. In your case, if it's unchanged, don't worry, keep doing it, and if you feel the need for the second round, please continue. Finally, you are going to feel awesome. So just trust the process and enjoy tapping.

The sequence I have shown is usually followed but if you want, you can tap randomly at any point. If you are in a public place or giving a presentation, you can tap on the base of your fingernails by stating your feelings or emotions at that moment. If possible, take a deep breath and allow yourself to relax. Alternatively, when I read "The Silva mind control method", I use certain hand gestures that I have programmed and I say, whenever I touch my index finger and thumb, I feel relaxed like a baby. To get a more profound and blasting effect, the combination of Ho'oponopono is even more amazing. While tapping on your points, chant Ho'oponopono, to get the magical feel. I used the combination of Ho'oponopono and EFT for my cravings and other amazing. The effect was much faster. You can customise the order of practicing these techniques depending on the situation. For example, you are willing to follow your healthy lifestyle, but in your home, that same lifestyle is not followed or your parents are not willing to feed you that, then start tapping and doing conversational Ho'oponopono. Like tapping on my points, "I'm sorry (your name) you are in this situation where you are not being given what you want to achieve your health goals", "please forgive me for feeling bad and upset about my parents", "thank you so much for recognising and healing the feelings within me", "I love you for taking care of me". Consider another situation where you don't have any motivation or willingness to do anything, like on a rainy morning or in the chilled winter. You are sleeping on your cosy bed with your blanket covering you entirely.

In this case, just lying on the bed, you start tapping on any point, be it your fingernails, or below the armpits and say your issue; I'm not at all feeling like getting up, I'm feeling lazy. Say whatever you are feeling, like you are telling your issue to your best friend. Slowly while tapping, you will automatically start tapping on other points and once you come in the right state of mind, chant Ho'oponopono. It will awaken the lion within you. Sometimes when you have junk food but later feel guilty, just tap at any point and instantly release that negative emotion of guilt. Once you master these techniques, believe me, you will be the master of your emotions, and whoever is the master of emotions, is the master of life.

By now, are you feeling confident and possible that yes I can do? Though Ho'oponopono and EFT are two different healing modalities, they are related to each other in one aspect. That one aspect is loving and accepting ourselves. Healing happens only when we are ready to forgive ourselves and accept ourselves. We are diseased, we are facing health issues solely because we are having some hard feelings against us. We need to release them, no matter what's the issue right now, we ourselves only are responsible for all of the issues in life. So my dear friend, be like a warrior and say yes I'm responsible for all the issues and I'm committed to releasing my negative emotions and allowing myself to feel confident, happy and relaxed. Once your mental room is cleaned, you are ready to decorate it, and furbish it with beautiful positive thoughts, which we will look into in our next chapter. Also, I will provide you with some tools to deal with the beliefs that stop us from feeling good about ourselves.

Key learnings to consider
In the festive season, we sweep out the dirt in our home and clean up the mess before decorating the home to look aesthetic. Similarly, negative emotions in our mental house are like the debris that remains after blasting or breaking the rock. The techniques of Ho'oponopono and EFT are powerful enough to clean up all our negative emotions and feelings and even clear our DNA memories. These techniques have countless testimonies of people who have transformed themselves to the next level and have cured themselves from seemingly life-threatening diseases. Our cravings are also emotions associated with the foods and hence can be released if we are willing to, and achieve the desired body shape. The resistance we often experience in taking action is often our beliefs formed with life experiences and societal conditioning. Be creative in addressing your problem. As such, when you get into the flow, you automatically tune into the script, but still, if you think you lack creativity, then tap for enhancing your creativity. Be a happy tapper creating magic in your and the lives of others.

Assignment
Assign a number 1-10 for your food cravings before practicing Ho'oponopono and EFT

____

Intensity rating after Ho'oponopono and EFT

____

Chapter 5

Living the life with new design

In this chapter, I will share some of my crazy techniques that actually produced results in my health and made me comfortable with what I am today. After cleaning my room, now I had a choice of my own as to what to buy and what to keep in order to design it in my way. I'm the architect of my mental house. In 3rd chapter, I introduced you to a powerful NLP technique where you learnt to blast the rock-hard cravings for junk food items. In this chapter, I'm going to introduce you to that same NLP technique for creating cravings for healthy food! I applied my own way to develop cravings for boiled food, but somewhere, I relate my way to this wonderful NLP technique.

Love to have it

In that chapter, I asked you to decrease the intensity of feelings and emotions for the food item. Here, you will do the opposite where you will increase the intensity for the unpleasant food that you don't like to eat. Now, imagine any food or vegetable like a bitter gourd that you absolutely don't like to eat, you repel it like the south and south poles of a magnet. The steps would be more or less similar but with a reverse game. Let's look into it.

Step 1: Close your eyes, and imagine bitter gourd (karela) kept on your table.

Step 2: Assign an arbitrary number from 1 to 10 based on your unpleasant experience. Let's say it's 1 or 2.

Step 3: Imagine the karela to be more unpleasant like its appearance, much more bitter taste, and smelling like medicine which you don't like and make it negative.

Step 4: Now get back to the original karela texture. Here you will notice a difference where your brain won't repel as it would earlier because the brain has learnt that the karela is somewhat better now.

Step 5: Imagine your favourite spicy foodstuff which you haven't considered releasing cravings. Let's take the example of kurkure.

Step 6: While imagining, make the cut karela a little bit crispy, and keep monitoring your feelings, assign a number to it.

Step 7: Make it more appealing by making the shape of karela like kurkure and tasting like a spicy tangy flavour. You should start salivating by now, assign a number here again.

Step 8: If you find it appealing then it's done, or else, make it further appealing by dipping in tomato ketchup sauce.

Step 9: Open your eyes and tease the wall in front of you.

Step 10: Now think of the cut karela pieces in front of you and recognise your feelings and emotions. Feeling like having it?

Now that you have gone through these steps, practice it every day for 5 minutes until you get programmed for having it.

Be vibrant and excited

In your house or mess (if you live in a hostel), you know what is to be cooked, then beforehand, you can practice this technique and tune in to some dancing to level up your energy because high energy brings you into a good mood. Keep saying this statement to yourself as a motivation as I said to myself "you look sweet when you have bitter and you look bitter when you have sweet". While having healthy food like sprouts, say in your mind, "ahh, yummy, these are so nutty", "I love having boiled stuff" "I enjoy munching on cut cucumbers, fruits that natural sweetness, ahh I just love it!" If any negative emotions appear, practice Ho'oponopono and EFT and you are ready to go. Tune into some exciting songs to dance and enjoy life. Some of my favourite songs I dance to before my meals are "Matteo Panama", "Twilight Zone", "Life Will Never be the Same", and some rocking Marathi, Punjabi, Haryanvi and Bhojpuri songs. I just want to gear up myself and be in the highest frequency mode. I don't go after lyrics, I just dance.

Use your physiology to transform your beliefs

Let's now discuss the beliefs that hold us back and stop us from enjoying our desired body shape. Many of us are scared to lose weight thinking we will become weak and also have saggy skin that will make us look ugly. Well, that might be true for some people, but there are countless transformations in the world where people have transformed their bodies to the next level. The main issue with our mind is, it enjoys focusing on negative aspects of life, and it finds joy being in that state. Our mind easily gets bored with positive things, but paradoxically, it wants to feel good. So what is the best way to stop the mind from focussing on the negative side? Whenever I faced this problem, I used to ask myself some questions. I've been doing this practice since 2019. Recall from Chapter 2, asking quality questions is an art that anyone can master. The time of lockdown was stressful for many of us, agreed? At that time, everything was closed; we were all confined like animals in our cages and people like me who are into fitness journey faced a hard time not being able to go to the gym. I was aware of my feelings and I thought, why not start to practice in my own confined room? Well, my mind was not ready. Guess why? Because I had a limiting belief that I could build muscles only in the gym, which I mentioned how to recognise in Chapter Two. Here is how I hammered my belief. My first hit was when I asked myself this quality question. Is this really true that people who don't go to the gym do have muscular bodies? Is this 100% true for every single person on this earth? That was an instant bulb-on moment, and my mind spoke to me, oh what a bullshit, get up and start in the room itself. Still, there was some resistance, then a second hit was required, to which my initial question gave an answer- change the body language or physiology. You might have experienced that whenever anybody with a lean body walks with chest and shoulders up, people comment sarcastically, "look, he is walking as if he's a champion bodybuilder." What happens at that time exactly? People's mind conceives from his physiology or body language that he is some champion or a Mr. Olympiad, but knowing the reality, they speak counter to what they conceived for justification or validation. This perception comes from the changes in physiology. So when you change your physiology, you generate the ability to bring any kind of desired emotion. In the earlier technique, I asked you to seek help from external sources to change your emotions. In this technique, use your physiology to create desired emotions. Recall that our emotions and habits stem from the beliefs we have, so if we keep feeling our desired emotions, it becomes possible to change our beliefs.

Let's assume you want to lose weight which is the hot topic of current day and age and you feel frustrated about it. You are overweight is the reality, but you feel frustrated is the emotion and you don't have direct control over your reality, but you do have direct control over your emotions. If you change that emotion and successfully be in that state, it's possible to exercise control over your reality. When I had my protruding belly, I had no direct control over my belly fat, then I changed my irritation by laughing like a kid whenever I see my belly in the mirror. In this way, my emotional state changed from irritation to fun which gave me the strength and power to work on it. Keeping that fun emotion, I used to giggle a lot while saying to my friends, "man no matter how much I eat, I lose weight and my waist size becomes like Korean teenage boys." Guess what, I became lean with my waist size going from 34 to 27! Around 2019, I wore jeans of size 34, and now, I'm wearing jeans of size 28. That too is loose on me. Believe me, I look like a teenager, even at 30+, my skin is glowing, I am youthful and my hair is fluffy, bouncy and voluminous. Believe me guys, you just command your body in the right state of mind; the body is ready to execute. This was the best proof in my life since I read Dr. Bruce Lipton's "The Biology of Belief" about how each and every cell of my body responds to my thoughts, feelings and emotions. Nowadays, I giggle by saying, no matter what I eat, I keep growing muscles a half an inch per day, then again giggling. Even though today I weigh just 56 kgs, I have an amazing definition of muscles, also being active, agile and stress-free. Importantly, when you are in that happy, joyful state of mind, criticism or negative comments from people don't affect you much, and you become a master of your life. Give it a try and make your lifestyle.

Relax, no assignment from my side in this chapter, you have put in your valuable efforts. Now, it's time to play. Whatever may be your goal, either weight loss, weight gain, or whatever belief you hold, refer to Chapter 2 and recognise your beliefs, release them and practice what you want with the right state of mind. I'm pretty confident you surely will see the results as I have seen in my life. If I had to discuss all my experiences personally face to face, it would take hours. Hence the main motive of my writing this book was to share my experience so that you also get the same desired shape of yours you have dreamed of.

Key learnings to consider
Our mind is not comfortable in being empty, it always needs something to think and feel. If we remove our habituated negative thoughts, the mind relaxes and looks for other thoughts, because it has its own cravings.

Therefore, it's necessary to feed our mind with empowering and joyful thoughts. In order to programme our mind, we take the help of our senses to imbibe positivity, and once we maintain that positive frequency within us, our mind gets habituated to it. Imagine how amazing life would become, just imagine how high your self-esteem would be. Tune into fun, exciting, joyful songs, praise yourself, give the taps of appreciation on your shoulders for achievements in your health. Move and be in the physiology of what you desire, keep that inner child alive by practicing body language; laugh, and smile like a baby. Welcome the new emotions in your life, your operating system has been successfully updated, congratulations.

The journey of transformation continues

I sincerely express my gratitude to you for considering this book as your companion in your own fitness journey. I apologize if I have missed something that did not relate to you and you felt incomplete or left out. I wrote this book not to give you in-depth knowledge about fitness, you already know it very well. This book was written to give you results that will be long-lasting and to make your process comfortable and joyful. Well, even if you felt you didn't find the answer to your question, just by practicing these techniques, you will upgrade to the next level regardless of your unidentified beliefs or emotional patterns. I will be happier to see you transforming your health, and my friend, this book is dedicated to your transformation, and your experience of results.

This is not the end of our journey, though this book is dedicated to cravings and body health, the techniques of NLP and Ho'oponopono plus EFT can be applied to all areas of your life. After mastering my health and fitness, I'm on the voyage of transforming my relationships, career and money status. So if you are willing to change other areas of your life, be it relationships, career or money, please reach out to me. It's the beginning of our journey together where I'm there to guide you with whatever I have learnt from my mentors and experienced in my own life, and how I'm transforming every day.

So my dear friend, congratulations on your desired body shape and eternal youthfulness with vitality and energy. Remember, we are always connected, we just need to dial the right frequency. In the near future, stay tuned for more powerful learnings about other aspects of life. Till then, keep transforming and be awesome, you are a sweetheart. Lots of gratitude and love to you.

To further continue your transformation journey, feel free to connect on:-

Youtube- Magical Mayur

Instagram- magical_healer_mayur

www.ingramcontent.com/pod-product-compliance
Lightning Source LLC
Chambersburg PA
CBHW031244130726
47988CB00008B/3232